Animals of the Night

BATS
AFTER DARK

Ruth O'Shaughnessy

Enslow Publishing
101 W. 23rd Street
Suite 240
New York, NY 10011
USA

enslow.com

Words to Know

colony—A group of animals that lives together.

echolocation—The process through which bats use sound to identify objects at night.

fertilizer—A substance that makes soil better for growing plants.

fossil—The remains of a plant or animal from millions of years ago.

guano—Bat droppings.

mammal—An animal that has a backbone, hair, usually gives birth to live babies, and produces milk to feed its young.

nectar—A sweet fluid produced by flowers.

nocturnal—Active at night.

pollen—Tiny grains from flowering plants that are needed for these plants to reproduce.

wingspan—The distance between the outer tips of a bat's wings.

Contents

A Close Encounter

Night has fallen and a group of campers sit by a fire telling scary stories. All of a sudden, a bat swoops by one camper's face.

Everyone screams and runs into their tents. They are afraid the bat might bite them to drink their blood or get tangled up in their hair.

But the truth is that the bat does not want to do either of those things. In fact, it has no interest in humans at all. The bat just wanted to eat the moth that flew close to the fire.

One of the campers peaks out of her tent and lets everyone know that the bat is gone. But people should know that bats do not want to hurt them, and they should not be afraid.

Winged Mammals

Bats are the only **mammals** that can fly. A mammal is an animal that has a backbone and hair. Also, mammals do not usually lay eggs. Almost all female mammals give birth to live babies, and they produce milk to feed their young.

Bats have been around for a long time. Scientists have discovered bat **fossils**, or remains, in Wyoming that are 55 million years old! Ancient bats looked very much like bats today. But experts think that the earliest bats could not fly. Instead, they may have glided through the air.

Fun Fact!

A bat's wings are really its hands. A layer of strong, thin skin connects the long finger bones to each other and to the bat's back and legs.

The long, thin bones in a bat's wings are its fingers.

Mega Bats

More than one thousand types of bats are found around the world. The two main groups of bats are the mega bats and micro bats. Mega bats are medium to large in size. There are more than 180 different kinds of mega bats. Most of them have long doglike snouts, large eyes, and small ears. They are usually found in the tropical areas of Australia, Africa, and Asia, where the weather is hot and rainy.

Fun Fact!

In China and Japan, bats are thought to bring good luck. The Chinese word for bat is *fu*. It means "good fortune."

In Vietnam, a young monk holds a mega bat. Its wingspan is about 3 feet (1 meter) across.

The largest mega bats are called flying foxes because their faces look like a fox's. The world's largest bat is the Malayan flying fox. Its body is about 2 feet (⅔ meter) long and when it spreads its wings, it has a **wingspan** of about 6 feet (2 meters). It can weigh up to 3 pounds (1½ kilograms), which may not sound like a lot, but it is big for a bat!

Fun Fact!

Male Malayan flying foxes have tufts of thick fur on their necks.

The Malayan flying fox is the biggest bat in the world!

Micro Bats

The other group of bats, the micro bats, are usually smaller than mega bats. Their faces look different as well. They do not look like dogs or foxes. There are also more kinds of micro bats than mega bats. Forty-seven types of micro bats live in the United States alone! But micro bats can be found throughout much of the world except Antarctica, the Arctic, and the world's hottest deserts.

Fun Fact!

The German word for bat is *Fledermause* (flay-der-maus), which means "flying mice." However, bats are not related to mice or any other rodents.

A scientist examines a Daubenton's bat, which belongs in the micro bat group.

The Kitti's hog-nosed bat is the world's smallest micro bat. It is found in the Southeast Asian countries of Thailand and Burma. It is also called the bumblebee bat because it is as small as a bumblebee. An adult bumblebee bat weighs around 2 grams, about as much as a dime. Its wingspan is under 6 inches (15 centimeters) across.

Fun Fact!

The Kitti's hog-nosed bat has extra webbing between its legs to help it fly better.

The Kitti's hog-nosed bat is no bigger than a bumblebee.

Different Diets

Most bats eat insects, but there are several kinds of bats that eat other types of food. Many mega bats eat fruit, such as mangoes, figs, and bananas. Others drink nectar from flowers.

Most micro bats eat insects, such as flies, mosquitoes, beetles, and cockroaches. There are also bats that eat fish, frogs, scorpions, spiders, small birds, lizards, and rats.

There are only three kinds of vampire bats. Two types mainly drink the blood of birds. The third kind of vampire bat bites mammals, such as cows, horses, mules, or pigs, for blood. All three kinds of vampire bats live in Central and South America.

Fun Fact!

One brown bat can eat about six hundred insects in an hour.

Vampire bats are the only
mammals that live entirely on
blood.

Nocturnal Animals

Bats are **nocturnal**, which means they are mostly active at night. They spend most of the day hanging upside down sleeping and grooming, or cleaning themselves. They take flight from the upside down position too.

Most bats hunt at night. Although the saying "blind as a bat" is very popular, it is not true. Bats are not blind, and some have very good eyesight. Bats also have excellent hearing.

While flying at night, some bats make high-pitched sounds. These sounds create echoes. The echoes let the bat know where different objects are. The echoes take the place of seeing the object. This is called **echolocation**. It helps bats hunt insects. A bat can find an insect up to 18 feet (5½ meters) away using echolocation. It even lets the bat know how large an insect is without seeing it.

A vampire bat flies at night. It uses
echolocation to find mammals to
feed on.

Bat Colonies

Many bats live together in large groups called colonies. Other bats may live by themselves or in pairs. A large colony can have millions of bats. The largest bat colony in the world is in Bracken Cave in Texas. Up to twenty million Mexican free-tailed bats may roost there during the summers.

While some bats live in caves, others make homes in old mines, trees, bridges, tunnels, and cracks in rock. They live in forests, fields, and near lakes, ponds, and streams. Bats are even found in cities.

In the winter, some bats migrate, or travel, to warmer places. Others hibernate, spending the winter in a deep sleep. This helps them to live through the winter when there is little food.

A bat colony rests in a cave in Bali, Indonesia.

Survival in the Wild

Bats have a few natural enemies. Hawks, owls, snakes, cats, and weasels will eat them . . . if they can catch them! When bats are not out flying, they roost, or sit and rest, in high or hidden places where many animals cannot reach them. Therefore, bats live longer than many mammals their size. Some types of bats live for more than twenty years. One type, called the little brown bat, can live up to almost forty years!

Fun Fact!

Giant hairy spiders called tarantulas eat bats!

This bat roosts out of the reach of predators in Brazil.

Family Life

Male bats have different ways to attract females. Some types sing, while others show off their wings or long hairs on their heads. After mating, the female bat will have babies, which are called pups.

Usually bats have one pup at a time. Yet some types of bats may have two or even four pups. Like all mammals, mother bats produce milk to feed their pups. Mother bats can tell their pups from all the others in a roost by their cry and their scent. Pups use their claws to hang onto their mothers while they roost or fly.

Fun Fact!

Some types of bats will bring food to an ill bat that cannot hunt. Female bats have also cared for bat babies whose mothers have died.

A baby bat clings to its mother as she flies.

Little Helpers

Bats help humans in different ways. Micro bats eat harmful insects that destroy crops and spread disease.

Bats that drink nectar also help the environment. When these bats sip a flower's nectar, pollen collects on their fur. When they fly to other flowers, they spread the pollen, which lets new plants grow.

Bats that eat fruit drop seeds as they feed. The seeds grow into new plants. Their droppings, called guano, also contain seeds that grow. Guano is useful to farmers, too, because it is rich in nitrogen, a colorless, odorless gas. This makes guano an excellent fertilizer for their crops.

Fun Fact!

Some bacteria found in bat guano can be used to make medicine.

A long-nosed bat eats cactus fruit. It also feeds on flower nectar and pollen.

Saving Bats

If bats are important to the environment, why are they in danger of disappearing? People are the biggest threat to bats today. In some places, such as tropical rain forests, areas have been cleared to make way for farms, houses, and towns. The bats that live there lose their homes and often die. Some people kill bats for food or because they think they are pests or evil.

In the United States, nine types of bats are at risk of dying out. These include the Florida bonneted bat, the Hawaiian hoary bat, and the Virginia big-eared bat.

Laws in some areas protect bats. However, these laws are not always obeyed. Some people have come together to protect bats. They protect the places where bats roost. They also have urged people to build bat houses in their yards. This would let bats safely roost. There are even bat rescue centers for injured bats.

A bat conservationist checks a bat box on a tree in England. Conservationists work to save animals from dying out.

Stay Safe Around Bats

As bats lose their homes in the wild, more of them may find shelter in people's houses and in buildings. Bats do not want to hurt people, but like with other wild animals, great care must be taken if you come across a bat. Bats can carry and pass on a disease called rabies. If someone with rabies is not treated quickly, that person could die. Very few bats get rabies, but it is best to follow these safety tips:

 Stay away from places where you know there are bats.

 Bats are wild animals. They can never be pets.

 Never touch a live or dead bat. Tell an adult if you see one.

 If you notice any holes or other openings in your home that a bat could enter through, tell an adult.

 If a bat is in your home, do not try to catch it. Tell an adult.

 Do not go near bat droppings. Tell an adult if you find guano close to where people are.

Learn More

Books

Hibbert, Clare. *Bat Hospital*. New York: Powerkids Press, 2015.

Markle, Sandra. *The Case of the Vanishing Little Brown Bats: A Scientific Mystery*. Minneapolis, Minn.: Millbrook Press, 2014.

Niver, Heather Moore. *20 Fun Facts about Bats*. New York: Gareth Stevens, 2012.

Zeiger, Jennifer. *Bats*. New York: Scholastic, 2012.

Web Sites

kids.nationalgeographic.com/animals/vampire-bat/
Read about the mysterious vampire bat.

animals.sandiegozoo.org/animals/bat
Learn fascinating facts about bats.

kidzone.ws/animals/bats/
Do fun activities like crafts and puzzles, look at photos, and discover more about bats.

Index

Published in 2016 by Enslow Publishing, LLC.
101 W. 23rd Street, Suite 240, New York, NY 10011

Library of Congress Cataloging-in-Publication Data
O'Shaughnessy, Ruth, author.
 Bats after dark / Ruth O'Shaughnessy.
  pages cm. — (Animals of the night)
 Summary: "Discusses bats, their behavior, and environment"—
Provided by publisher.
 Audience: Ages 8+
 Audience: Grades 4 to 6.
 Includes bibliographical references and index.
 ISBN 978-0-7660-6752-3 (library binding)
 ISBN 978-0-7660-6750-9 (pbk.)
 ISBN 978-0-7660-6751-6 (6-pack)
 1. Bats—Juvenile literature. 2. Nocturnal animals—Juvenile
literature. 3. Animal behavior—Juvenile literature. I. Title.
 QL737.C5O84 2016
 599.4—dc23
          2015009968

Printed in the United States of America

Portions of this book originally appeared in the book *Bats: Hunters of
the Night.*

Photo Credits: Alex Joukowski/Moment/Getty Images, p. 23; Dr.
Merlin Tuttle/BCI/Science Source/Getty Images, p. 27; Gavriel
Jecan/Photodisc/Getty Images, p. 21; Geostock/Photodisc/Getty
Images (vampire bat), p. 1; Johner Images/Getty Images, p. 19; Joel
Sartare/National Geographic/Getty Images, p. 5; kimberrywood/
Digital Vision Vectors/Getty Images (green moon dingbat); Mike
Powels/Oxford Scientific/Getty Images, p. 29; narvikk/E+/Getty
Images (starry background); NHPA/SuperStock, p. 13; Peter
Charlesworth/Light Rocket/Getty Images, p. 9; Rexford Lord/
Science Sourse/Getty Images, p. 17; Roberta Olenick/All Canada
Photos/Getty Images, p. 7; samxmed/E+/Getty Images (moon
folios and series logo); © Steve Downer/ardea/age fotostock, p. 15;
Thomas Marent/Visuals Unlimited/Getty Images, p. 11; Wassana/
Mathipikhai/Shutterstock.com, p. 25; Yves Adams/Stone/Getty
Images, p. 3.

Cover Credits: Geostock/Photodisk/Getty Images (vampire bat);
narvikk/E+/Getty Images (starry background) kimberrywood/Digital
Vision Vectors/Getty Images (green moon dingbat); samxmeg/E+/
Getty Images (moon).